KNOW
YOUR
CAPABILITIES

KNOW
YOUR
CAPABILITIES

GEORGE
BARNETT

KNOW YOUR CAPABILITIES

Copyright © 2015 by George Barnett

The ClearLake Group

San Francisco - Boston - New York - Singapore

www.theclearlakegroup.com

Library of Congress Control Number: 2014919034

ISBN: 978-0-9909227-0-4 (paperback)
ISBN: 978-0-9909227-1-1 (ebook)

Designed by AuthorSupport.com

Printed in the United States of America
By IngramSpark (Lightning Source)

CONTENTS

INTRODUCTION

S ome of you probably have participated in your own company's annual business planning process, or the 3 year plan, or the 5 year plan.

Maybe you brought in one of the major strategy consulting firms to help you. Maybe your in-house corporate strategy group or M&A group did most of the work.

Either way, you have an existing approach and infrastructure for strategic decision-making. And it looks something like what you see in Graphic 1 below.

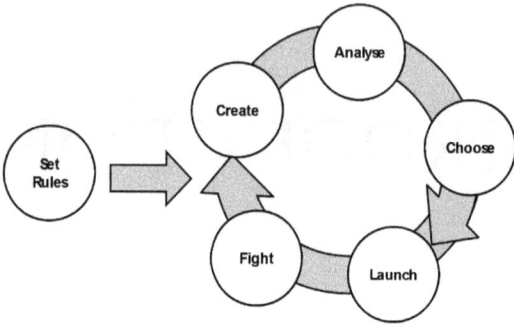

Graphic 1: Your existing approach to strategy

Set Rules	Devise and agree upon the rules of engagement (who can participate and how, the timeline, scope, decision-making criteria, inputs, etc.)
Create	Brainstorm the heck out of the room to generate as many clever ideas as any crowdsourced effort claims to do
Analyse	Narrow down the list using your favourite mix of quantitative and qualitative tools
Choose	Use your governance rules to choose the winning option
Launch	Hand over the instructions for implementation to the rest of the firm, typically managed by a temporary project team
Fight	Spend the next year fire-fighting implementation issues and internal resistance

Then repeat the entire cycle in year two.

And what does this process typically look like? A group of 5 to 10 confident, creative people in a boardroom, spurred on by the enthusiasm, instincts, and charisma of their chief executive, seizing upon the new idea on the whiteboard...

The new strategy. The new direction for the firm...
"We will become the Apple of shoe retailers."
"We will become the Alibaba of Africa."
Et cetera.

And just like a group of studio executives in Hollywood, they don't really know if their choices have any chance of success. Their instincts tell them to follow. In fact, there is even a respectable corporate strategy called "fast follower" that many of them were taught in business school.

What they weren't taught in business school, one of the dirty little secrets of corporate strategy, is that most strategies fail. Fail miserably.

Why? The decision-makers rarely, if ever, take the time upfront to think through what they realistically can accomplish and execute successfully.

With their own people, their own resources, and with their accumulated intangibles, such as processes, culture and innate knowledge. Factors that, when put into action, we call the capabilities of the firm.

FOR EXAMPLE, TAKE
HONEYWELL INTERNATIONAL

Most of us think of Honeywell as a manufacturer of systems and electronics equipment, an also-ran to the legendary GE, one that was nearly acquired by GE in 2001. The simplest path for Honeywell's executives historically has been to watch and imitate GE.

The only problem with such a path is that Honeywell is not GE. Not even close.

Fortunately, a new executive team at Honeywell realised this, and reflected on Honeywell's own distinctive characteristics. Honeywell is particularly good at nurturing a fiercely-held culture, and has a proud history of growing successful businesses around their reputation for being customer-centric and creative. Management decided to build and expand upon this culture to include behaviours tied to continuous improvement, in effect using Honeywell's cultural capabilities to de-risk the implementation of their new strategy, "the Honeywell Operating System".

The irony underlying the premise of this book is just how much investment in the form of research and analysis typically goes into the strategy process of a Fortune 500 firm, only to be disappointed with the result.

And how do they end up with such disappointment? There are two reasons.

REASON #1 – THE ERROR OF TOO MUCH NOISE, NOT ENOUGH SIGNAL

By not deliberating on what are your capabilities, you set yourself up for failure by incorporating unnecessary risk and uncertainty inherent to the open-ended, unconstrained process of discovery within the second step (Create).

After all, whoever said that any company can do anything under the sun? We don't make that claim about individuals, do we?

> **Whoever said that any company can do anything under the sun?**
>
> **We don't make that claim about individuals, do we?**

There's a reason why we don't find jockeys who are six feet tall, or professional basketball players under six feet in height.

There's a reason why there are so many lawyers in regulated industries, why there are so many military veterans in supply chain logistics firms, and why there are so many former athletes in sales.

REASON #2 – THE ERROR OF FALSE POSITIVES AND FALSE NEGATIVES

By not explicitly including the influence of existing capabilities on the probability of successful execution, you are prone to misrepresenting (through optimism or pessimism) the risk and uncertainty in your financial projections and models of the strategic options under consideration at the third step (Analyse).

Because, no matter how you view strategy, some things serve as starting conditions, upon which you can reasonably invest for future growth. Despite the claims of some to the contrary, you can't simply go out and acquire capabilities "off the shelf" from other firms. It's too easy to believe in the fallacy of instant, problem-free integration.

For, in the end, firms are simply groups of people, sometimes large groups of people, and as such they are governed by aspects of human nature and behaviour. The members of a firm, either individually or collectively, are able to get certain things done or not. And, on average, you can figure out in advance what those do-able things are.

That "figuring out" is the piece of analysis we suggest adding to your existing strategic decision-making process (see Graphic 2 below).

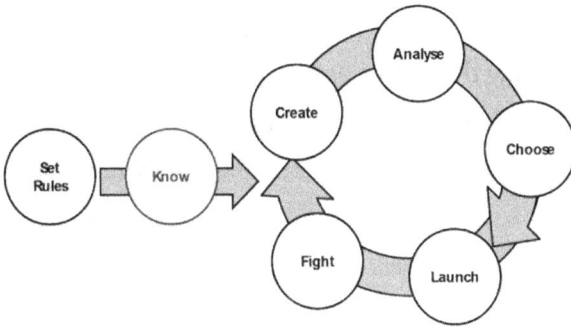

Graphic 2: A better approach to strategy

The easiest analogy is that of DNA and genetics: the presence or absence of a particular gene does not definitively predict an outcome, but it does tell you the relative likelihood that some outcome may or may not happen, given a certain environment.

If you are not a carrier of the CFTR mutation for cystic fibrosis, chances are you won't develop the disease. If you are a carrier, and you mate with another carrier, then there is a much higher likelihood that your offspring will develop the disease.

Similarly, if the capabilities of your firm do not include a proclivity to design innovative products, then chances are you will struggle to deliver on an innovation-based strategy.

Even if you acqui-hire one or two dozen start-ups out of Silicon Valley (sorry, Yahoo! and eBay).

Some commentators go so far as to describe companies as if they have some form of corporate DNA, or distinctive way of doing things that goes beyond culture. We refer to this "DNA" as their set of capabilities.

And, if you don't take the time to know your capabilities, you will make decisions without the benefit of the simplest piece of data available to you.

> **If you don't take the time to know your capabilities, you will make decisions without the benefit of the simplest piece of data available to you.**

In this book, we set out the provocative case that your success depends on knowing your capabilities and building that knowledge into your decision-making models.

Not provocative in the sense of stating something for the first time.

After all, the idea of knowing one's self goes back in history all the way to the temple of Apollo and the oracle of Delphi (if not earlier), and has been used as a call to reason ever since.

"To thine own self be true..."
(Polonius, in Shakespeare's Hamlet)[1]

No, provocative in the sense that we give it the prominence it deserves.

Call it the re-balancing of our inner reason, or impulse for intellectual order, with our inner impulse for chaotic creativity. Both deserve a fair hearing in strategic decision-making.

Like so much else in leadership studies, academics have barely scratched the surface of what really goes on inside the minds of CEO's and other executives tasked with major strategic decisions. There exists an ongoing tension between logical thinking and the thinking that appeals to emotions and instincts. And this is especially the case in circumstances associated with creativity and growth.

To address this tension, this book starts with our findings on what we call "the universal reference set of capabilities", independent of industry and geography. We then share with you some examples of firms that have demonstrated awareness of their capabilities at some point in time, and examples of others that clearly have not.

Finally, we challenge you to create a truly great strategy for your firm. The starting point is building your awareness of your company's capabilities, referring to industry data and the growing literature on the benefits of individual and group awareness in the workplace. To help you in this effort, we include a do-it-yourself toolkit of 4 simple steps that you can add to your existing strategy process.

> **We challenge you to create
> a truly great strategy.**

As a bonus, we have added an appendix outlining more detailed capabilities-related exercises, along with an invitation to participate in the ongoing global research initiative, Know Your Capabilities.

CHAPTER ONE

The Universal Set of Capabilities

A mbiguity drives me crazy. It's the opposite of clarity, and, if nothing else, the aim of this book is to make some things perfectly clear. Like,

Not understanding capabilities is the #1 culprit of strategic failure.

Don't take our word for it. The research bears this out.

Every company has a corporate strategy, yet most corporate strategy efforts fail to achieve their expected results.

For example, most corporate change efforts since 1981

have fallen far short of the sustained results they set out to accomplish (by two-thirds to three-quarters, depending on whose consulting report is cited).

Take the most glaring example, the failure rate of M&A strategies. In their new book, "Masterminding the Deal", academics Peter Clark and Roger Mills found that possibly two-thirds of all M&A efforts fail (i.e. the effort did not deliver the results promised when the deal was announced). Clark and Mills attribute this to irrational exuberance leading to the buyer overpaying for the target company. Quite often, this occurs later in the business cycle, when what we witness are cases of "strategic or transformational" mergers, terms used when a company buys its way into an unfamiliar business (i.e. does not have the capabilities for success).[1]

Add to this evidence the recent study by Leinwand and Mainardi, in which they point out the fact that "few strategies explicitly mention capabilities at all."

They cite a few examples of what they refer to as coherence between a company's capabilities and its strategy (Wal-Mart, Pfizer, Coca-Cola, P&G), noting these examples as rare exceptions to the rule.[2]

Round out the argument with the investigations of Sheth and Sisodia into the reasons for corporate failure and success. From their analysis, they conclude that companies succeed because, by chance or circumstance, their internal capabilities and assets seem to match the opportunities in the environment at that particular time. Alternatively, they can just as easily fail if they prove unable or unwilling to change their culture, processes, systems and structure. This phenomenon, variously described as the dominant logic, active inertia, or blind spots, is the prime cause for decline and failure, the authors argue.[3]

We explore this further in chapter three.

A capability means more than just a skill or a competency.

The word "capability" is used in so many different ways that it creates confusion.

Like eBay CFO Bob Swan, speaking recently about M&A strategy, "If somebody else has a competency or a capability, that if we acquire now it will be quicker than building it..., that is an important aspect of whether to buy or build."[4]

You can buy a person, a team, or a product. You cannot buy a capability.

This confusion can leave you prone to making serious strategic mistakes.

A more helpful definition of a capability is the ability to get something done through the interplay of multiple elements of your business acting in concert.

For example, a defined business process for launching new products is a skill or element, whereas the ability to create and launch compelling, differentiated products over and over again is a capability.

At ClearLake, we believe that every capability is like an ecosystem — an interdependent network of tangible and intangible elements in a company's business environment. That environment may lie wholly within the organisation's boundaries, or it may encompass other players in its network of suppliers, partners, and customers.

> **A defined business process for launching new products is a skill or element, whereas the ability to create or launch compelling, differentiated products over and over again is a capability.**

Some capabilities are relatively simple, reliant on only one or two elements. Others consist of several highly interdependent elements. What all capabilities have in common is their systemic effect beyond a single functional area, often company-wide.

Our research and client work have demonstrated that you can usefully categorise the underlying elements of business capabilities into six areas: Community, Culture, Motivation, Technology, Work Streams and Knowledge (see next page).

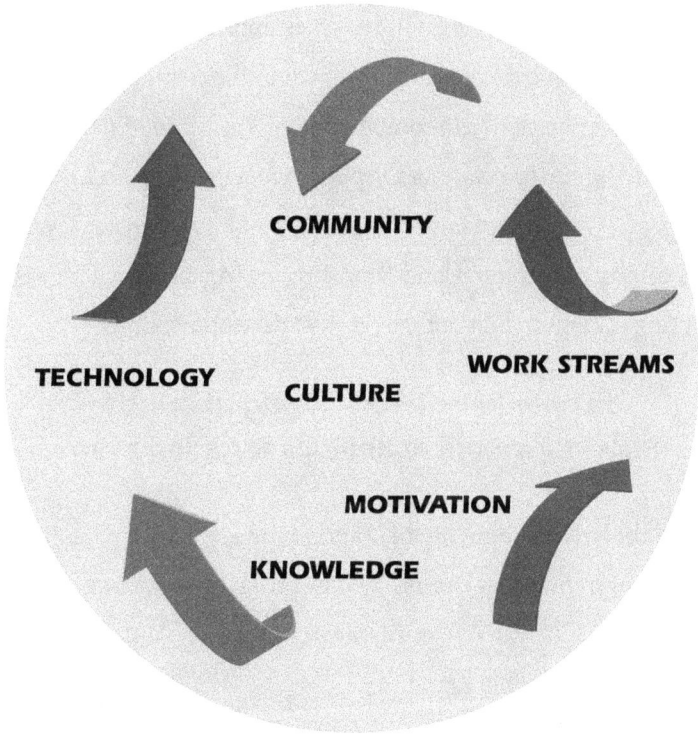

Community	Culture	Motivation
The social and informal life of the organisation	The personality of the organisation	The underlying reasons people do things
Technology	**Work Streams**	**Knowledge**
The application of science, engineering and design to advance the organisation	The structural and procedural ways that work is done	The wisdom, skills and information accumulated by experience and education to benefit the organisation

Using the above capability as an example, we would describe "the ability to create or launch compelling, differentiated products over and over again" as a combination of Motivation (in this case, the willingness to iterate, or the passion for iteration), Technology (e.g. an ongoing exploration of the limits of, say, material science in display technology), and Workstreams (e.g. creating and nurturing the repeatability of the product development process).

People have been talking about the importance of capabilities for a long time.

Scholarly treatment of (and support for) capabilities theories of business enterprise dates back at least to the work of Alfred Chandler (e.g. his books: Strategy and Structure (1962), The Visible Hand (1977)).[5]

Chandler made the case that firms could excel by building organisational capabilities over the long term.

Then, in 1990, Prahalad and Hamel popularised the idea of core competencies and their role in strategy, giving further impetus to management researchers to explore and explain how an understanding of innate abilities contributes to business success.[6]

Some researchers emphasise the relationship of capabilities with customer value propositions, and others the relationship with competitive advantage. Some delve into the dynamic nature of capabilities, and still others the social or relative aspect of putting capabilities into practice.[7] [8]

Others, like Van der Heijden, refer to the characteristics of an organisation ("the business idea") and the degree of fit necessary for a good strategy to succeed.[9]

There has not been a simple way to use capabilities in strategy. Until now.

Such a simple tool needs to address head-on the cognitive tension mentioned earlier, i.e. the tension between your inner reason and your instincts.

In nearly every strategy exercise that we've observed, there is a moment when a gut check is performed on the results of the analytics.

The data points one way, but your heart points in another direction. What do you do?

Just like SONY, the once-mighty Japanese electronics manufacturer, with next to no market share in smartphones globally, but still pursuing the premium-branded segment in the United States, destroying shareholder value along the way...

One of our clients, a banker, referred to this inner struggle as the search for "the secret sauce". Well, we believe that we have found the ingredients...

There exists a universal reference set of capabilities, independent of industry sector or geography.

This reference set of capabilities provides an overarching framework or language for understanding what underpins a company's success.

From the earliest days of the ClearLake Group, we have focused on what has become our passion and purpose: unleashing the global power of capabilities.

We have become avid and inexhaustible purveyors of information on this topic through our role as, and our network of, researchers and strategists.

Our starting point was our collective reflections on the total quality management (TQM) movement, and its parallel search for industry databases of quality indicators (QI's). We noted how these QI's were often independent of any specific industry, let alone country or region of origin.

From that observation came the hypothesis that the same must be true for capabilities. At some level of abstraction, a capability becomes universal. So we set ourselves the task of identifying those universal capabilities, the ingredients, so-to-speak, of a company's "secret sauce."

> **At some level of abstraction, a capability becomes universal.**

We launched the Know Your Capabilities global research initiative to codify and categorise the universal set of capabilities, along the way noting the firms that appear to be aware or not of their capabilities over various periods of time.

To date, numerous global firms, operating executives, and opinion leaders have contributed to this study, which has emerged as an invaluable resource in the field.

The Know Your Capabilities initiative is by far the most comprehensive capabilities study ever conducted. No other program to help global strategists align strategy and capability with business growth has ever been conducted on this scale.

OBJECTIVES

- Develop capabilities-based insights and solutions for effective global corporate strategy decision-making
- Create an overall approach that is practical and experience-based
- Create a fact-based foundation for thought leadership
- Build a community of excellence

APPROACH

- More than 10 years of structured research and solution development
- Numerous global firms involved
- Numerous in-depth interviews at global, regional and local levels
- Numerous respondents in the Know Your Capabilities database

In this chapter, we introduce this universal dataset for the first time, as a definitive reference for business executives and their corporate strategists.

The dataset consists of approximately 100 capabilities, ranging from:

The ability to touch the consumer emotionally

to:

The ability to change dysfunctional routines

These capabilities span the corporate value chain, encompassing all functional areas and aspects of management.

In general, you can think of capabilities in four broad categories:

1. Some firms focus on **what they know**, with their capabilities tied to some form of knowledge asset.

2. Others focus on **what they make**, with their capabilities tied to a mix of R&D, manufacturing, and administrative assets.

3. Still others focus on **how they sell**, with their capabilities tied to their approach to customers, competitors and costs.

4. And others focus on **who they are**, with their capabilities tied to the identity of the firm.

Examples of capabilities, by category, are shown below:

What they know	**What they make**
The ability to...	The ability to...
• Improve operating cost efficiencies	• Translate technical know-how into new product markets
• Understand what to do and what not to do	• Push the limits of design
• Manage conflicts of interest with customers	• Cannabilise one's own products

How they sell	**Who they are**
The ability to...	The ability to...
• Change from a product-focus to a customer-focus	• Translate values into durable behaviours
• Touch the consumer emotionally	• Change dysfunctional routines
• Extend a company's brand halo	• Manage operations for the long term

Any one capability may sound patently obvious, but the secret to knowing your capabilities lies in identifying the unique combination of 4 or 5 capabilities, the company's set of capabilities, that together underlie your success.

Every company has its own inherent sub-set of these capabilities, upon which it draws consciously or unconsciously for its success.

Over the past two decades, we have worked with hundreds of companies of varying sizes, business models, and geographic footprints. In most cases, very little effort is required on our part to uncover at least one or two capabilities, which are often considered common knowledge or part of the company's folklore. More careful attention and effort are needed to tease out the remaining capabilities, especially those dependent on the contribution of disparate parts of the firm, or those whose full potential has yet to be realised.

In our experience, no two companies are alike in terms of their capabilities.

Interestingly, in our experience, no two companies are alike in terms of their capabilities. They may share one or two capabilities in common, but, over time, they have found dif-

ferent ways to capitalise on those through the involvement of
distinct third, fourth, or even fifth capabilities.

And, given all the different combinations of capabilities
theoretically possible, the uniqueness of each firm is not that
much of a surprise.

Over the next few chapters, we make the case for why you
should care.

CHAPTER TWO

Examples of Firms and Their Capabilities

M ost firms, at some point in their lives, take advantage of their capabilities to grow and succeed in their marketplaces.

At the same time, we've learned about the myth of persistence, from first-hand experience and from discussions with a wide range of operating executives. As Walter Kiechel aptly put it, "Exemplary corporate performance—as in 'consistently beats market averages' or 'invariably delivers on promises'—doesn't last."[1]

Somewhere along the way all firms stumble, even the most exalted, having forgotten what got them there in the first place. For a fortunate few, they take steps to regain an understanding of their capabilities, and re-claim their former, or even greater, success.

> **Somewhere along the way even the most exalted firms stumble, having forgotten what got them there in the first place.**

The most poignant example is that of Apple, and much has been written about Apple's changing fortunes across the periods of leadership by Steve Jobs, John Sculley, Steve Jobs (act II), and now Tim Cook.

But there are other examples, like Honeywell International, which appears, under the leadership of David Cote, to be surpassing its earlier period of glory. And the jury is out on whether the return of A.G. Lafley will allow P&G to soar once again, or whether the re-privatisation of Dell by founder Michael Dell will amount to much. Remember that Jerry Yang's late stage two year stint as CEO of Yahoo! didn't deliver the expected results...

Let's continue our exploration of capabilities by looking at firms at a time when each clearly knew their capabilities, based on the testimonial of executives who worked there.

As a reminder, one can think of capabilities in four broad categories:

1. Some firms focus on **what they know**, with their capabilities tied to some form of knowledge asset.
2. Others focus on **what they make**, with their capabilities tied to a mix of R&D, manufacturing, and administrative assets.
3. Still others focus on **how they sell**, with their capabilities tied to their approach to customers, competitors and costs.
4. And others focus on **who they are**, with their capabilities tied to the identity of the firm.

Firms draw their unique set of capabilities from across the categories. Some examples are below, drawing upon our research and experience:

What they know	**What they make**
• Thomson Reuters • Samsung Group	• Nokia • Pixar Animation Studios • Honeywell International • Samsung Group
How they sell	**Who they are**
• Advanced Info Service • Honeywell International • Samsung Group	• Nokia • Advanced Info Service • Pixar Animation Studios • Honeywell International • Samsung Group

Let's take a look at these companies in detail, touching upon when the companies demonstrated one or more of their capabilities.

NOKIA

Our first example is known today primarily for their decade-long success as the world's leading mobile phone handset manufacturer, propelled by widespread adoption of the GSM standard. Enter the iPhone and, well, Nokia's handset business now belongs to Microsoft.

I first encountered Nokia in the course of my work in the global pulp and paper industry in the late 1990's. I was fascinated that the same company could be pre-eminent in such different industries.

In fact, Nokia's origins lie in the mid-1800's, when Fredrik Idestam founded his first pulp mill as Nokia Ab. For over a century, Nokia applied its capabilities, related to what they make and who they are, to a series of industrial breakthroughs (rubber processing, electronics, power generation), culminating in the decision to focus on mobile telephony and the internet.

What has Nokia done, at times, so well? Certain characteristics have been documented and accredited to them a number of times. The ability to change and move quickly (understandably, given their legacy of industries)... Being savvy businesspeople, strong negotiators, and, interestingly, taciturn, that is, in how they communicate. They don't talk much unless they have to.

As one of the first serious players in the mobile phone handset business, they recognised quickly that they were "sitting on a gold mine, on unlimited demand" (so to speak). That meant they would have to move quickly. They drew upon their strengths in mass production to manufacture phones as quickly as possible: at peak, 17 phones per second, shipped out of South Korea on 747's. Sound like today's iPhone mania?

Another example of their moving quickly occurred in the context of their rivalry with Ericsson. In 2001, Ericsson was making mobile phone handsets considered superior to those of Nokia (smaller, better features). In reaction to a fire at a Philips components plant in New Mexico, one that supplied critical radio frequency chips to both Nokia and Ericsson, Nokia's supply chain leader moved quickly to secure a series of lock up agreements with competing parts factories globally, in effect freezing Ericsson out of the market.

Ericsson soon reversed its risky sole source supply chain strategy, but the damage was done. Ericsson's market share continued to drop, and, in 2014, Ericsson exited the market, selling to SONY its share of the SONY Ericsson mobile phone joint venture.

At the same time, some insiders point to Nokia's capabilities in global product development, specifically the ability to synchronise complicated development programs across time zones and cultures, finding a common culturally-accepted language, communications, and methods to build and deliver complex products.

And Nokia's ability to innovate. Who remembers now that, before any other player, Nokia was the first to bring to market a camera-phone in a small device?

> **Who remembers now that, before any other player, Nokia was the first to bring to market a camera-phone in a small device?**

Closely tied to these capabilities is their sense of global product management, balancing global needs with local needs. When defining a product as well as making product changes during development, Nokia believes that it takes local requirements into account, rolling out a sometimes identically-tailored and sometimes locally-adjusted product based on common elements. They therefore build for global release, rather than multiple disconnected local releases.

They even emphasise the importance of this capability by encouraging and rewarding employees to take and seek input from other, often remote, locations before proceeding with their work, with the goal of reducing ambiguity in the knowledge that other locations would approve the product.

However, this set of capabilities proved to be insufficient for the long term. We referred earlier to Nokia's storied savvy negotiating abilities and taciturn nature in communication. When combined with the rest of their capabilities (speed, product development, innovativeness), being taciturn can play out as stubbornness. And sometimes being stubborn pays handsome returns, for example when, at the same time as they were churning out millions of handsets, they were bold enough to invest nearly a billion dollars to build out the necessary back end infrastructure to support the growing network needs for backhaul, transport, security, etc.

Tellingly, that same stubbornness spelled disaster, especially when it came to adjusting to an important local market, the United States. As a result, Nokia, in several important instances, misread indicators in the US market, leading to their exit from the handset business in 2014.

For example, in 2002, Nokia decided not to launch a flip-phone in the US market. Leadership of Nokia's US affiliate urged Nokia's global leadership to make the move, but the response was, "No, we don't believe in flip-phones. We don't do that form factor." That left an opening for Motorola to grab share with the RAZR line, and, even more strategically critical, to win the hearts of the all-important carriers AT&T, Verizon, Sprint, and T-Mobile.

Which meant, when Nokia followed up in 2006 with the N-series (including the N93 with the innovative feature of the first WiFi chips inside handsets), the US carriers refused to carry them. Redesigning the product line without WiFi meant a delay of 6-12 months and the ongoing loss of momentum in the US market.

So that by the time Steve Jobs was shopping around the concept of the first iPhone, he was able to dismiss the carriers' concerns about its WiFi chip with his confidence in one of Apple's capabilities, its understanding of what wins the hearts of consumers. In this case, the characteristic of stubbornness was coupled with a mutually beneficial capability. AT&T alone met Apple's terms initially, and the rest is history.

> **In Apple's case, the characteristic of stubbornness was coupled with a mutually beneficial capability.**

Now, it's not that Nokia didn't know about touchscreens. Far from it. Once again, its stubbornness kicked in. "Nokia does not believe in touchscreens. Haptic interfaces are the way forward. Users want to feel the buttons."

Contrast that with Apple's point of view, stemming from its depth in user experience design: "Users don't care about feeling buttons. It just slows them down. If you can use the phone faster, you can do more."

A lot more.

Some wags joke that, in Nokia's Finland, you couldn't use a touchscreen with mittens on.

Meanwhile, in the US, Nokia executives themselves began to buy iPhones and ditched their Nokia handsets...

THOMSON REUTERS

The second example from our research is the self-described "world's leading news and information company." With origins dating back to 18th century London (Reuters) and early 20th century Canada (Thomson), Thomson Reuters grew into the behemoth it is today through the savvy use of changing technologies in media.

Now, some observers, including insiders, describe today's Thomson Reuters as a firm that struggles to do things well. The one area of exception is their structured and disciplined investment process, both for M&A and organic growth purposes.

For, as a media conglomerate, Thomson Reuters comprises many businesses and sub-businesses. It evaluates each on the same basis, with a balanced and prioritised decision-making process, using the evaluations as input to their investment strategy.

Crucially, they then have convinced themselves that they are equally capable in the task of post-merger integration, drawing upon the knowledge gained in the acquisition process.

However, their track record demonstrates that they are

more successful in the case of small- to medium-sized acquisitions, like the recent takeovers of CRSTL Solutions and Pricing Partners SAS in 2013. The ongoing challenges facing Thomson Reuters itself, more than 7 years after Thomson acquired Reuters, speak to the limits of their ability to integrate acquired firms.

In the next chapter, we discuss how a company like Thomson Reuters can use such knowledge, such organisational self-awareness, to risk-adjust their financial projections.

ADVANCED INFO SERVICE

The third example, this time from our client experience, looks at the carrier side of mobile telephony in south-east Asia. Advanced Info Service PLC (AIS) is the largest mobile phone operator in Thailand.

A critical capability, focusing on how to sell, was AIS's ability to identify and take advantage of the inefficiencies of the telecoms market in Thailand. Founder Thaksin Shinawatra learned where the big opportunities were, how to open up the political process (how to win a licence), etc. In other words, the carrier game.

Building upon AIS's simple origins in the 1980's as a computer rental business, Shinawatra secured a 20 year monopoly concession in analog mobile phone services and the rest was, well, history. For those who follow Thai politics, they will understand the controversial role Shinawatra has played and continues to play in Thailand.

Telecommunications is a controversial utility in any country. For AIS to maintain their franchise rights to sell services, they had to know whom they needed to bring in, and how to manage the government and the military, amongst other stakeholders and vested interests.

In terms of a second capability, AIS has a keen sense of who they are, creating a distinct company culture. Shinawatra's business values were relatively modest (by industry standards), stemming from his regional influences in northern Thailand, as well as his educational influences (a PhD in criminal justice from Sam Houston State University).

As a result, some say, he deliberately hired people who were very talented and not from the powerful Thai families (e.g. the CFO, Pong-Amorn Nimpoonsawat, was an orphan), despite Shinawatra's own roots within the Thai aristocracy in Chang Mai. In this way, he legitimised entrepreneurialism for many, and employees at AIS were empowered to make decisions within a more decentralised organisation.

AIS legitimised entrepreneurialism for many, and empowered employees to make decisions within a more decentralised organisation.

Such a culture is considered atypical in Asian corporations, and it remains an open question if the culture will be sustained under the ownership of Singapore's Temasek.

PIXAR ANIMATION STUDIOS

The next example, from our research, starts with capabilities related to who they are and how that drives what they make. Yes, we are talking about a creative company, in this case, Pixar (now part of the Walt Disney Company).

Pixar's origin story dates back to the late 1970's as a unit within the computer division of Lucasfilm. The Graphics Group, as it was known then, was founded on the cutting-edge computer graphics work of Ed Cattmull and his peers at the New York Institute of Technology.

From the beginning, across many chaotic years within Lucasfilm, as an independent firm under the leadership of Steve Jobs, and then as an autonomous studio within Disney, Pixar has relied upon Cattmull's understanding of the critical role of talent in the newly-digital creative business.

Cattmull nudges his people to come up with projects consistent with the story-telling traditions of Hollywood, while rewarding them in the manner of Silicon Valley. His overall objective is to nurture a team that can tackle interesting problems and solve them, in essence the ideal mix of artists and engineers.

Even more to the point, he and his fellow founder John Lasseter, the chief creative officer, then drew upon a second capability of Pixar, the ability to adapt compelling ideas from external sources.

Pixar began as a computer imaging hardware company, and, from these roots, Catmull explored how some of the principles of creativity were embedded within hardware manufacturing. In particular, he gave Toyota Motor Company credit for turning its company into a creative firm by engaging its people in problem-solving.

> **Catmull gave Toyota credit for turning its company into a creative firm by engaging its people in problem-solving.**

Perhaps partly because they were so far removed from Los Angeles, whose studio culture can be suffocatingly inward-looking, Pixar was able to look far afield (in this case, Japan), to Toyota and its approach to continuous improvement and respect for people. In adapting "the Toyota Way" to animation film production, Pixar built a collaborative work environment (the Braintrust) that is highly conducive to the types of positive criticism and shared responsibility that some credit for their distinctive art-form.

Just as Toyota encouraged constant feedback from its line workers to reduce errors, Pixar opened up a system of constant feedback to uncover problems and source input from across the firm.

Trying to balance these capabilities related to what they make with those related to who they are, all within an overarching Disney culture, continues to provide a healthy challenge to the founders of Pixar.

HONEYWELL INTERNATIONAL

The fifth example, from our research, is a classic turnaround story, in which a once-great company rediscovers its capabilities and returns to the top of its game: the engineering giant, Honeywell International.

The original Honeywell dates back to the late 1880's Minnesota and the first inventions of Albert Butz in new heating technologies and control systems. These were later combined with the heat generation inventions of Mark Honeywell, along with a series of acquisitions in industrial controls.

Towards the end of the 20th century, Honeywell had expanded into a wide range of businesses. Despite a reputation for engineering creativity (a legacy of long-time CEO W.R. Sweatt) and for being customer-centric, Honeywell suffered from being sub-scale and unproductive relative to its competitors. In quick succession, the much larger Allied Signal acquired Honeywell, and the even larger General Electric attempted to acquire the successor firm (named Honeywell).

The latter deal was blocked on antitrust grounds, leaving Honeywell with an uncertain future.

Enter a new CEO, David Cote, a protégé of GE's Jack Welch, who quickly decided that a new Honeywell culture was necessary. Similar to the situation at Pixar, he found that Honeywell was adept at customising ideas from external sources (ironically also "the Toyota Way", only this time calling it the "Honeywell Operating System" or HOS). As a result, productivity has soared, along with product quality and employee safety and job satisfaction.

In addition, to deal with the conglomerate sprawl, he introduced the discipline he learned at GE of entering and exiting markets decisively ("Great positions in good industries" is a current motto). For example, Honeywell sold its consumer auto-products division, and doubled down on speciality-materials and building controls.

The financial markets have responded accordingly, with Honeywell's shares outperforming the S&P 500 index over the past decade. Some would call this a vote of confidence that Honeywell will use its renewed understanding of its capabilities as it makes its next set of strategic decisions.

SAMSUNG GROUP

Our sixth example, also taken from our research, is of a different type of conglomerate, the largest chaebol or South

Korean conglomerate: Samsung Group. Its size and complexity stagger belief.

Founder Lee Byung-Chul started Samsung as a trading company just prior to World War II, but it wasn't until the end of the Korean War that Samsung took off, in tandem with the government's all-encompassing modernisation efforts. Some would say that the history of Samsung is deeply entwined with the success of those efforts.

Today, Samsung is known worldwide for its leadership in electronics, including Android phones, flash memory components, and flat-panel televisions. But its interests span far beyond those of Samsung Electronics to include market leading positions in shipbuilding, construction, and life insurance, to name a few.

Insiders will tell you that, if you look at the company, its real strength is its people and its distinctive culture. Samsung, more than other big Korean firms, is militant, with a rigid, top-down culture. They've been able to attract excellent people and strong leaders, who motivate their employees to give physically their best to the firm.

For many outside observers, Samsung is very odd, and hard to understand. A critical aspect of any culture is the story-telling around the culture. One apocryphal tale at Samsung is the 1993 Frankfurt Declaration ("Quality first, no matter what."). Chairman Lee Kun-Hee took 200 executives and asked them to change everything in their lives (except kids and spouses), due to the then-poor state of quality of Samsung products.

Drastic changes occurred. Not only is there a story here, but Samsung also erected a memorial building to this moment, including furniture from the hotel in Frankfurt.

In effect, some say, Chairman Lee declared bluntly that "design is important and we are terrible at it", going on to create the Samsung Design Institute, investing heavily in the design of future products.

Fast forward 20 years to 2013, and Samsung has declared its intentions to enter new businesses essential to society. These businesses include LED lighting, electric-vehicle batteries, medical devices and other green-tech and healthcare areas.

To succeed at this, Samsung will have to draw upon its history of scaling capacity quickly and profitably, as it did in liquid-crystal displays and flash memory. It may also draw upon its proclivity to follow and imitate market leaders, rather than entering markets first. As a result, to Apple's consternation, Samsung is its most important supplier as well as its toughest competitor.

> **To Apple's consternation, Samsung is its most important supplier as well as its toughest competitor.**

Which brings us to Samsung's capabilities related to what it knows. For the past 5 years, Samsung has been second only to IBM in being awarded patents in the United States. Its roots are both in the developing world and the industrialised world, giving it particular insight into the products and services demanded by global consumers. Samsung's ability to operate truly globally delivers both tremendous scale as well as footholds in the fastest growing economies.

THE COMMON ERRORS IN KNOWING CAPABILITIES

But, as we mentioned at the start of this chapter, just because a firm knows its capabilities at some point in time, that doesn't mean it always will. In a way, "the price of success is eternal vigilance."

The price of success is eternal vigilance.

In fact, in the examples we've just described, in each case the company exhibited an understanding of one or two capabilities, not necessarily the full complement.

In our experience, there are four common errors that companies make in the interplay between capabilities and strategy.

The Four Common Errors in Knowing Capabilities

1. Those who knew at one time, and then forgot
2. Those who thought they had a capability, but did not
3. Those who are unaware that they don't know their capabilities
4. Those who had one capability, but lacked other critical capabilities

Let's address each in turn, with examples.

1. Those who knew at one time, and then forgot

Ironically, given the myth of persistence, and how dynamic truly competitive marketplaces can be, a company that appears to know its full set of capabilities at one time may no longer.

In our experience, we have seen many great companies forget their capabilities as they make new strategic decisions. A particularly poignant example from our client work is UBS, the pre-eminent Swiss financial services company formed out of the merger of the Union Bank of Switzerland and the Swiss Bank Corporation in 1998.

For a long time, observers would say that UBS (and their predecessor constituent firms) did know at least some of their capabilities. They knew how to protect their wealth-management clients, and they were rock solidly prudent, sober, and risk averse.

But, in response to the changing regulatory environment for the financial services industry, UBS, under the leadership of Marcel Ospel, made fateful strategic decisions that ran counter to these capabilities.

Just like some of their competitors, they bought their way into new lines of business (e.g. hedge funds, including Dillon Read Capital Management) that promised higher returns at higher risk (in the never-ending search for yield), believing that they were buying the concomitant capabilities to run those businesses.

And along the way they forgot their own motto: "If you don't understand the business, don't do it." When the 2008 financial crisis hit, UBS suffered unprecedented losses as a result.

> **Along the way, UBS forgot their motto: "If you don't understand the business, don't do it."**

2. Those who thought they had a capability, but did not

From our research, we often observe that companies can, and do, become victims of their own mythologies, telling themselves that they are good at certain things without putting those beliefs to rigorous testing.

Take SONY, for example. Like Nokia, they too believed in their ability to innovate, not just imitate, doggedly pursuing its big ideas against the doubters of the world. And they had a moment in time in which the SONY brand was one of the most valued in consumer electronics.

However, as the internet became central to the industry, the set of capabilities needed to innovate shifted decisively away from the SONY model of insularity to a model predicated on networks of strategic alliances. Just look at how Samsung and Apple inter-relate. SONY has yet to demonstrate the willingness or ability to engage in such relationships.

Such a capability includes being open to disruptors and influential customers such as the developers who hacked into SONY's robot dog Aibo. Over the past decade, while immersed in the Silicon Valley tech startup world, I have yet to bump into SONY as a serious player, either in terms of strategic investor or alliance partner. Unlike so many of their tech peers, SONY has no accelerator or corporate venturing arm in the Valley.

It remains an open question if SONY has learned from the past decade and deepened its understanding of its true capabilities, as it attempts to turn around its consumer electronics business.

3. Those who are unaware that they don't know their capabilities

Remember Donald Rumsfeld? He made famous the conundrum that sometimes you don't know what you don't know.

We've seen this dilemma in action firsthand in our client work, including at SingTel, billed as Asia's leading communications group. Even insiders describe the company as one that has yet to fulfill its undoubted potential by remaining blissfully unaware of their capabilities.

SingTel makes an enormous amount of money as a holding company, as you would expect from its monopoly within Singapore, but it doesn't know what to do with it. There is not enough trust within the firm for people to share and talk openly. There are good financial dashboards providing lines of sight, anything that typical business analytics can provide. What they can't measure is what is inside the heads of their employees.

SingTel may be an interesting ASEAN player but they are not a global leader. Why, for instance, does Western Union still handle funds transfer for them? Like the scene from the movie "On the Waterfront", observers mutter "You could have been a contender...", a world-class player. Instead SingTel remains a resource-rich monopolist, in effect a sovereign wealth fund.

> **Instead, SingTel remains a
> resource-rich monopolist, in effect
> a sovereign wealth fund.**

Some say it is cultural in nature. At the formation of Singapore, cash was a rough and dirty proxy for success. It was SingTel's duty to create a new and better world. And now? Without knowledge of its capabilities, SingTel underperforms.

In other cases, we've seen publicly-traded companies begin to embark on a corporate strategy (e.g. a roll up or acquisition-based consolidation play in the food and beverage industry), only to have us point out that they lacked fundamental capabilities necessary for success (in this example, the ability to identify targets, close deals, and integrate the acquired companies). Fortunately, we caught them in time, before significant shareholder value was destroyed.

4. Those who had one capability, but lacked other critical capabilities

Each company possesses a set of capabilities, and these capabilities work in concert. A common error then is to have a deeply-embedded awareness of one capability and to over-attribute success to that one, rather than exploring and understanding the full set.

Boeing is a great example (from our research) of a company

with insight into one of its capabilities, and at the same time being unaware of how that capability works best in combination with others, i.e. in sets or systems.

The brilliance of the new 787 Dreamliner design arose from Boeing's undisputed mastery of pushing the limits of design while bringing innovative new products to market. However, after their merger with McDonnell Douglas, a new emphasis on risk-aversion and cost-cutting led to challenges in getting approval for innovative projects like the Dreamliner.

Looking to Dell for inspiration, Boeing believed that they could outsource the majority of the process of bringing the new airplane to market, what they referred to at the time as the reinvention of manufacturing.

A clever strategic idea, with one hitch: Boeing did not have Dell's capability to make effective use of networked external resources. And we are not just talking about the manufacturing of parts along a global supply chain. In this case, Boeing outsourced the design, engineering and manufacturing of entire sections of the plane to more than 50 strategic partners.

In the end, the Dreamliner project budget overshot by billions and the timeline was, let's just say, not up to competitive standards, with missed deadlines and retrofitting the norm.

From my client work, I remember the same concept, i.e. outsourcing or hollowing out the entire core between basic research and sales, being pitched to companies in a host of industries, when the idea was popularised in the 1990's. In no instance was the importance of capabilities to execute such a strategy given the prominence it was due.

A pity.

Another example from our client work is that of Hewlett Packard. In the early part of the 2000's, management was struggling with what more they could do with their army of engineers employed in printer technology. These engineers, located in Oregon, were bringing out the latest and greatest technological innovations in printing. And, at the time, over 100% of HP's profit came from the sale of printer ink, which meant that everything else they were doing was losing money. How could they get ahead of the curve in new target markets?

They came up with a myriad of ideas but were unable to decide amongst them. The challenge remained that their cashflow continued to come primarily from printer ink. How long was this sustainable?

> **HP knew they were good at some things, but they didn't know how to translate those things into newer areas.**

HP knew that they were good at some things (e.g. the material sciences, mechanical and electrical engineering aspects of the printer business), but they didn't know how to translate

those things into newer areas. They lacked the translation capability. They couldn't break down their one capability into
the elements necessary in order to act on them in new ways.

It's not that the individuals themselves lacked knowledge,
or skillsets, or work processes. I remember during this time, I
was in venture capital in Palo Alto and was approached by one
rogue team of engineers within HP's printer business. They
were frustrated by the internal obstacles (like timing, resource
allocation, and decision rights) to funding and supporting pi-
lot projects geared towards testing innovative ideas related to
their inkjet technology intellectual property.

Not only couldn't HP develop the ideas in-house, but they
were hesitant to allow their own people to spin out the ideas
into start-ups in the best traditions of Silicon Valley. Ironic,
given HP's iconic place in the history of Silicon Valley.

Yet another example from our work concerns one of the
largest fish processing and packaging firms in the US Pacific
north-west. Their new private equity owners had achieved a
series of cost efficiencies and were looking to grow the top line
with a new growth-oriented corporate strategy. The premise
was to take advantage of a key capability that they had already
identified, i.e. knowing how to package and process seafood.
And the default path was to bring that capability to new customers in new geographies around the world.

Fortunately, before embarking on that path, they exam-
ined what other capabilities would be needed to be successful

in those other geographies, including supply chain logistics, regulatory, and taxation concerns. Without the full set of capabilities, the risks involved meant that their projections of potential upside had to be adjusted. They then could make a better-informed comparison of the relative merits of alternative strategic options.

In summary, all of these are examples, from our research and our experience, of companies knowing or not knowing their capabilities. We'll explore the implications of these examples in more detail in the next chapter, in which we make the business case for knowing your capabilities, and outline what you can do about it.

CHAPTER THREE

The Business Case, and The Simple Steps to Follow

I n 2009, Microsoft opened its first retail stores in Arizona and California, in response to the success of the Apple stores. Yet, Microsoft had never in their history demonstrated the direct, intimate engagement with end-users for which Apple is famous.

How on earth did they convince themselves that they could just conjure up this capability out of thin air? By hiring someone?

Contrast the empty feeling when you walk into a Microsoft store with the excitement you feel as you enter an Apple store.

This is the height of hubris. You cannot pretend to be what you are not.

Hence the central theme of this book: the importance of your organisation taking a critical look at itself and asking the question – what are we capable of doing?

By knowing your capabilities, you gain clarity. You can then take the next step of combining the clarity gained with the judgment of your executive team, to generate your new strategy.

We believe in having clarity rather than certainty. Achieving certainty is near impossible and, in the least, a waste of resources. Rather, you should gain clarity about your capabilities – a useful and practical way to resolve the anxiety of addressing your strategic challenges.

> **We believe in having clarity rather than certainty. Achieving certainty is near impossible and, in the least, a waste of resources.**

In this chapter, we first make the case that you should want to know your capabilities, by answering these six straight-forward questions:

Six Questions to be Answered

```
┌──────────────┐     ┌──────────────┐     ┌──────────────┐
│ What do we   │     │              │     │ Don't        │
│ mean by      │ ──▶ │ Awareness    │ ──▶ │ companies    │
│ clarity?     │     │ of what?     │     │ do this      │
│              │     │              │     │ already?     │
└──────────────┘     └──────────────┘     └──────────────┘
                                                 │
                                                 ▼
┌──────────────┐     ┌──────────────┐     ┌──────────────┐
│ What to do   │     │ What         │     │              │
│ about it?    │ ◀── │ happens as   │ ◀── │ Why don't    │
│              │     │ a result?    │     │ they?        │
└──────────────┘     └──────────────┘     └──────────────┘
```

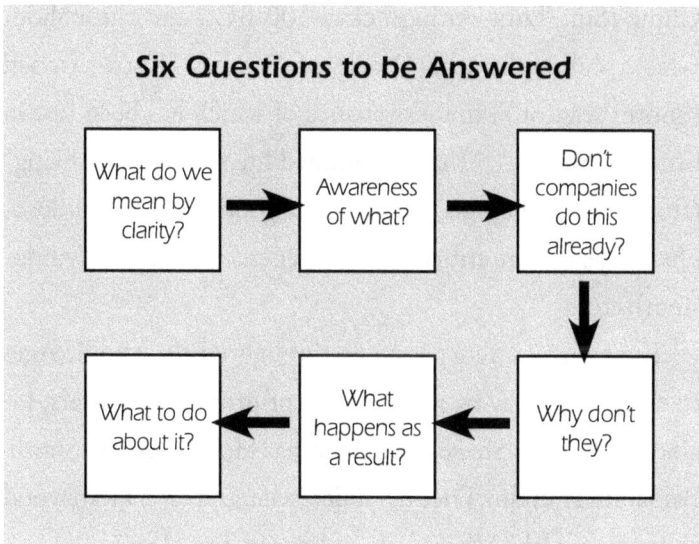

WHAT DO WE MEAN BY CLARITY?

By clarity, we mean: as much awareness as realistically possible, on an organisational level.

In a practical way.

Expending resources within reason.

Exercising judgment as to the balance between evidence and intuition.

The foundation for building awareness is having an appreciation for knowledge and its uses. From the earliest oral and written records, people have identified the importance of self-awareness.

Examples can be found from ancient Egypt (proverbs inscribed within the Luxor Temple, circa 1400 BC), ancient

China (Sun Tzu's writings, circa 500 BC), and throughout Greek philosophy (the Oracle of Delphi's "Know Thyself (gnothi seauton)", the provenance of which has been lost in history); Socrates' "The unexamined life is not worth living" (from Plato's Apologia); Plato's "The good life of the philosopher depends on critical self-awareness" (from the Symposium), etc.

These themes were passed on throughout the Middle Ages to the present day by a who's who of prominent writers, including William Shakespeare, Thomas Hobbes, Adam Smith, Benjamin Franklin, Friedrich Nietzsche, and even Hollywood scriptwriters (the Wachowski siblings in The Matrix).

The majority of awareness literature has focused traditionally on the individual level, especially as applied to interpersonal dynamics and conflict resolution.

However, more recently, some have begun to draw connections between self-awareness and social awareness, citing the work of Daniel Goleman et al.[1]

	Personal Competence (how we manage ourselves)	**Social Competence** (how we manage relationships)
Recognition	**Self-Awareness** • Emotional self-awareness: reading one's own emotions and recognising their impact; using "gut sense" to guide decisions • Accurate self-assessment: knowing one's strengths and limits • Self-confidence: a sound sense of one's self-worth and capabilities	**Social Awareness** • Empathy: sensing others' emotions, understanding their perspective, and taking active interest in their concerns • Organizational awareness: reading the currents, decision networks, and politics at the organisational level • Service: recognising and meeting follower, client or customer needs
Regulation	**Self-Management** • Emotional self-control • Transparency • Adaptability • Achievement • Initiative • Optimism	**Relationship Management** • Inspirational leadership • Influence • Developing others • Change catalyst • Conflict management • Building bonds • Teamwork and collaboration

How does this connection between self-awareness and social awareness work in practice?

In our experience, we've helped companies raise the emotional intelligence of their individual leadership team members and middle managers, and to bring those changes to bear on broader organisational behaviours.

In one example, the supplementary objective of the effort was to nurture the broader organisational capability "to change dysfunctional routines" across a company's Asia-Pacific regional organisation.

We contend, therefore, that organisational awareness is incomplete without taking into account the social dimension (what we refer to as the Community elements of capabilities).

And by social, we mean the full range of interpersonal relations, such as the role of political appetite to achieve greater ends, how power is exercised by people at all levels to engender good will, the degree of affection towards the organisation as a whole and to each other, the passion, the innocence and the disposition of good will towards each other, etc.

Remember, from chapter two, how stubbornness translated into success or failure at Nokia and Apple, depending on its interplay with one or more capabilities of each firm?

For many leaders, awareness of these aspects is intuitive and rarely explicitly researched, analysed or addressed. We believe that some companies exhibit capabilities that include these dimensions. For those companies, creating a shared explicit awareness of these capabilities is an essential part of the strategy process.

AWARENESS OF WHAT?

Capabilities.

What we referred to earlier in this book as an interdependent network of tangible and intangible elements in a company's business environment, both internal and external.

There is a finite set of capabilities, and every company has its own inherent sub-set, which it uses to differentiate itself in the marketplace.

Knowing your capabilities means doing more than a SWOT analysis, a relative competitive landscape, or a situational analysis. Those tools are useful inputs to the corporate strategy process, but are insufficient on their own. The addition of a capabilities analysis provides the basis for execution risk-adjustment, when projecting the range of potential benefits and outcomes accruing to different strategic options.

> **Knowing your capabilities means doing more than a SWOT analysis, a relative competitive landscape, or a situational analysis.**

Knowing your capabilities does not require an IT-based knowledge or performance management system, or big data analytics. Insights from such internal systems can inform how senior management views company performance over time, but the design of such intelligent systems typically aims for predictive outcomes, with the goal of certainty at the expense of clarity.

DON'T COMPANIES DO THIS ALREADY?

No, they do not.

Throughout our research, we have found that most operating executives agree with the principle of knowing capabilities in order to build and implement successful strategies. Those same executives admit that few companies, if any, do so in any consistent manner.

Possibly, they haven't had simple enough tools at hand. Or perhaps their gut tells them that it just isn't as important as other input factors to their strategic decision-making.

Imagine what would happen if we ran other organisations like that, organisations that are completely dependent on talent. Like sports teams. Or the military.

Not so comforting, is it.

You should put as much care into knowing your capabilities as you do knowing any other aspect of your business, whether it be your financials, your logistics, or your contractual obligations.

Don't take our word for it. Look at the management literature.

Recall from chapter 1, that Leinwand and Mainardi found that "few strategies explicitly mention capabilities at all."[2]

They cite a few examples of what they refer to as coherence between a company's capabilities and its strategy (Wal-Mart, Pfizer, Coca-Cola, P&G), noting these examples as rare exceptions to the rule.

> **You should put as much care into knowing your capabilities as you do knowing any other aspect of your business.**

In 2012, Mainardi went on (along with colleagues Adolph and Neely) to examine the positive impact on shareholder value of knowing your capabilities in M&A strategies.

"The results of (our) study suggest that a CEO — generally used to relying on financial considerations in evaluating M&A — should look every deal prospect up and down from a capabilities perspective. This lens isn't used often enough, perhaps because capabilities are not on the strategic radar for many companies, either in the boardroom or on Wall Street. They are seen as functional matters, not as fundamental levers of value creation that can make the difference between success and failure for a corporate direction."[3]

When it comes to strategy, unfortunately the reality is that most talk about the importance of knowing capabilities, but few actually put in the necessary effort.

WHY DON'T THEY?

As we pointed out in the introduction, there exists a continuous tension between inner reason and instinct within the minds of most leaders. This tension very often results in putting to one side the logic of knowing (and having) capabilities, for the sake of following gut instinct.

This leaves most companies prone to the errors of false optimism and false pessimism.

For example, there is "the capability as commodity" fallacy, resulting in what we call in Silicon Valley the tendency to do "IFTTT".

IFTTT (pronounced "ift" as in "gift") stands for "IF This, Then That", a simple but powerful tool popular amongst software developers as a recipe for connecting two disparate digital activities.

For example, you can tie a trigger like "if a person tags a photo on Facebook" with an action "then send me a text message."

In strategy, we too often see this form of IFTTT: a company realises it lacks a certain capability necessary for a given strategy, so it goes out and buys it. "If my company lacks a capability, then I can just buy it."

This is the "capability as commodity" fallacy, an underappreciation of just how difficult it is to build and maintain a capability for the long term (let alone attempt to buy one and expect it to flourish within your firm).

Some recent M&A deals illustrate this fallacy well (think Nike buying Umbro, Vivendi buying Activision, the Washington Post acquiring Forney, Eisai buying MGI Pharma, Yahoo! buying Tumblr, etc., etc.).

Some observers believe that one of the main reasons for the failure rate in M&A is missing capabilities and the reflex reaction of back-filling.

And this fallacy is just one response to the challenge of managing a company for the long term. Any investment geared towards boosting a firm's long term competitive position will come into conflict with the forces demanding short term profits. Companies that are in it for the long haul recognise that capabilities are not commodities. They are, in effect, "the secret sauce" of the firm, as that banking CEO earlier put it.

> **Companies that are in it for the long haul recognise that capabilities are not commodities.**

To everyone's credit, there has not been, until now, a simple way to bring capabilities into the analytics of corporate strategy. Remember, it wasn't until Michael Porter introduced his five forces that companies included competitive factors in their financial models on a consistent basis either.

For there is an information asymmetry between a company's financial system and its systems for understanding capabilities. Even corporate talent systems, one element of capabilities, are at an early stage of quantification. But, as Billy

Beane demonstrated in his management of the Oakland A's baseball team, there is progress being made in how companies challenge assumptions about talent, in terms of what it can and should be.

WHAT HAPPENS AS A RESULT?

Your risk of failure goes up.

And at the best of times, risk is under-appreciated. During times of strategy formulation, executives are urged to suspend their disbeliefs, in the search for new sources of growth.

"Risk is often poorly understood within companies and … commonly used analytical tools, such as net present value, can lead companies to misunderstand their situations and come up with bad strategies."[4]

As we pointed out at the outset of this book, every company has a corporate strategy. And most companies actively manage their corporate strategies, with updates and major changes on a regular basis. Yet most corporate strategy efforts fail to achieve their expected results.

For example, most corporate change efforts since 1981 have fallen far short of the sustained results they set out to accomplish (by two-thirds to three-quarters, depending on whose consulting report is cited).

Take the most glaring example, the failure rate of M&A strategies. In their new book, "Masterminding the Deal", academics Peter Clark and Roger Mills found that possibly two-thirds of all M&A efforts fail (i.e. the effort did not deliver the results promised when the deal was announced). Clark and Mills attribute this to irrational exuberance leading to the buyer overpaying for the target company. Of those deals that are successful, "the likelihood of a deal delivering economic benefits is greatest when the goal is to cut costs by merging two similar firms."

Contrast this with the case of "strategic or transformational" mergers, terms used when a company buys its way into an unfamiliar business (i.e. does not have the capabilities for success).[5]

The record-breaking acquisition of WhatsApp by Facebook in early 2014 is a case in point: proponents make the claim of this being strategic or transformational (the chance for Facebook to reach a large new market, per CEO Mark Zuckerberg), whereas naysayers criticise Facebook for overpaying for the company (potentially $19B for a company with annual revenues of $20M).

Regardless of your position on the deal, within months Facebook began to revise publicly the strategic rationale as the internal contradictions between Facebook Messenger and WhatsApp became problematic.

And, just as M&A activity occurs in waves, the admission of errors associated with specific M&A deals (in the form of write-offs of goodwill) occur in waves, with a time lag of up to 5 years later.

So keep an eye on Facebook's quarterly earnings reports in late 2018 / early 2019...

And that's not all that can go wrong.

Organisations too often fail at strategy execution.

Various sources have reported implementation failure rates at between 60 and 90 percent. A Bain Consulting study of large companies in eight industrialized countries found that seven out of eight companies failed to achieve profitable growth between 1988-1998, defined, rather modestly, as 5.5% annual real growth in revenues and earnings, with returns that exceeded their cost of capital. Interestingly, 90% of the companies in the Bain study had strategic plans with targets exceeding these growth targets; few achieved them.[6]

Other studies point to an alarmingly high failure rate of business initiatives.

Unilever, for example, embarked upon its well-publicised Path to Growth strategy in 2000. Since then, it has not only failed to grow profitably but has also seen its European sales decline. Part of the problem was being slow to address emerging market trends, such as the one for low-carb diets.

Similarly, Volkswagen embarked on a burst of growth in the late '90s by acquiring other well-known automobile brands, only to find that these began competing against each other as competition intensified by the middle of the decade.[7]

And, as Paul Ormerod noted: "Failure is (a) fundamental feature of human social and economic organisations... In

America, more than 10 per cent of all companies fail every year, with more than 10,000 closing every week."[8]

As observed in chapter 1 by Sheth and Sisodia, companies succeed because, by chance or circumstance, their internal capabilities and assets seem to match the opportunities in the environment at that particular time. As such, they can just as easily fail if they prove unable or unwilling to change their culture, processes, systems and structure. This phenomenon, variously described as the dominant logic, active inertia and blind spots, is the prime cause for decline and failure, the authors argue.[9]

One area of blind spots, per Bossidy and Charan, is the lack of realistic evaluation (by senior-level leaders) of whether an organization can effectively implement its new strategic plan.[10]

Homburg (et al.) stress that, at the core of a successful approach to strategy implementation is the recognition that different types of capabilities, organizational processes, and systems need to be adjusted in order to implement the selected strategy.[11]

And Frigo is adamant that implementation cannot succeed unless the strategy itself is designed to be executable, and the execution will not result in outstanding performance unless it is designed around the goal of maximizing financial value.[12]

And so, according to Schaap, despite investments in week-long retreats, extensive marketing research, and expensive outside consulting services in developing strategic plans, unfortunately, many of these plans do not come to fruition, because of inadequate design or poor implementation.[13]

In short, by not knowing capabilities, companies increase the risk and uncertainty in the financial projections and models of their strategies, leading to the high failure rates observed in business strategies.

> **By not knowing capabilities, companies increase the risk and uncertainty in the financial projections and models of their strategies.**

In contrast, knowing your capabilities builds for you a risk-adjusted approach and a more powerful basis for financial decision-making.

One that is more powerful than what is usually employed.

WHAT TO DO ABOUT IT?

In the remainder of this chapter, we describe for you a Do-It-Yourself toolkit for how you and your company can have a greater chance of success, by building awareness of your company's capabilities.

Remember our central argument: that your strategy process should begin with building an awareness of your capabilities.

Identifying, articulating and mapping these capabilities are critical inputs to the strategy process. When capabilities are well-articulated, the executive team can take into account the implications for strategic opportunities available to their firm.

For your strategy team, we suggest using a simple 4-part toolkit.

1. Identify the capabilities of your firm

Through the use of internal surveys and interviews (one-on-one, focus groups), you can tap into the collective wisdom of your employee base. Be sure to diversify your pool of potential respondents to include both relative newcomers as well as long-term employees with the knowledge of the company's heritage, employees with contrarian points of view, and representation across functional areas, business units, and geographic regions.

2. Calculate how well each of your strategic options fits with your capabilities

Once you have created your strategic options, assign sub-teams to each option.

Charter each strategic option team with a capabilities self-assessment of fit, at the same time as you have them generate the first set of financial pro-formas. Layer on top one or more methods to compensate for bias, for example, demands for supporting evidence and/or testimonials from subject matter experts.

3. Make risk-adjustments based on degree of fit

Combine the financial projections prepared for each strategic option with the relative degrees of fit generated in the previous step. In effect, you weight, or adjust, the projected sales and costs over time with the risks of execution. Depending on the level of detail of your financial projections, you may choose to weight individual underlying drivers of sales and costs.

CONSIDER THIS EXAMPLE, FROM NIKE

If you have a certain set of capabilities but not others, and if you have a specific business goal to meet, what are the implications? You know that here is what you can and what you cannot do. Should you therefore build or buy the capabilities that you lack? Does this approach place constraints on your new strategy?

Nike has a strong brand and culture, and it gets in the way of their efforts to integrate acquisitions successfully. They repeatedly bring nice brands in-house, add the Nike brand to them, and then they fall apart. It has been a series of failures.

To obtain a capability that you may be lacking involves effort and may affect the success of your new strategy. Weighting or risk-adjusting the projected financials associated with the strategy dimensionalises the idea and makes sense to executives. You help them with the process of elimination of strategic options.

For example, some companies (cf. Thomson Reuters) are better at integrating SME-sized acquisitions than large-scale acquisitions, and thus they should use different probability of integration success factors depending on the scale of the target being acquired.

4. Reinforce the process through corporate governance

Instruct your Board of Directors and other key decision-making bodies to insist upon capability-level analyses when asked to assess strategic recommendations. In addition, the Board should hold the CEO accountable for the company knowing its capabilities, and propagating this knowledge throughout the firm.

Which brings us full circle.

By having your strategic team incorporate this straightforward 4-step toolkit into their existing strategy process, you will in effect risk-proof your strategy against the main culprit of strategic failure.

For capabilities are merely a means to an end, that is, getting to your new strategy.

Every strategist wants to generate the next powerful strategy for their firm. They have their strategic options. And they have their financial analyses. They just need to connect the two through the sobering chemistry of capabilities.

We leave you with this easy-to-remember metaphor: think

of your capabilities as the battery that drives powerful strategy, as illustrated below.

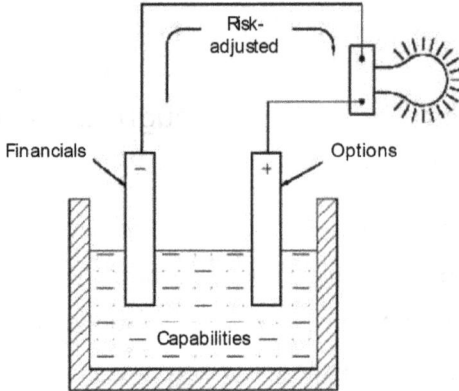

Graphic 4: The Capabilities Battery

**Think of your capabilities as the
battery that drives powerful strategy.**

CONCLUSION

The central premise of this book is that, yes, every firm has its own inherent set of capabilities. And it is through using and investing in these capabilities that each firm succeeds in the marketplace.

In Chapter One, we introduced you to the universal set of capabilities, the approximately one hundred ways that companies get things done through a combination of factors related to Community, Culture, Knowledge, Motivation, Technology, and Workstreams.

Most companies have only a few capabilities that really

matter to surviving and thriving. These essential capabilities lie at the heart of how a firm operates and creates value.

When taken together, these capabilities can be thought of as a capability ecosystem. They differentiate the organisation. They are often both sustainable over time and difficult for others to replicate, since they are integrated and interdependent, i.e. they build upon and reinforce each other.

So, does this mean that companies competing in the same industry and markets will share the same set of capabilities? That is highly unlikely.

Every organisation grows its own combination of capabilities to make it viable, based on how it evolves over time. That implies different starting conditions and a different set of external and internal influences.

In Chapter Two, we demonstrated that no company is persistently good at anything (notwithstanding the proverbial "search for excellence"), and choices are made – consciously or unconsciously, as the external and internal environments change – throughout the firm's life to achieve success.

Success will mean different things to different companies: a level of influence, a certain size or scale, a sustained growth rate, a great work environment, or a targeted profitability. Whatever the measure, it is the dynamic combination of capabilities that underlies its success.

Then, in Chapter Three, we made the argument that your strategy process should begin with building an awareness of your capabilities. Otherwise, your risk of failure is unnecessarily high.

We then provided a simple 4-part toolkit for identifying and articulating the effect of these capabilities, as critical inputs into your strategy process.

In closing, we invite you to join the growing community of practitioners around the world who, either out of necessity, passion, or curiousity, are expanding their strategic methods to incorporate knowing capabilities.

In the appendices section, we include further resources to aid in this effort.

APPENDIX

Clearlake Resources for
Building Awareness of Capabilities

To help you build awareness of the capabilities of your firm, the ClearLake Group offers four resources: the database of capabilities, a set of exercises, a range of custom workshops, and a community of practitioners.

Let's take each in turn.

1. The **database of capabilities**, answering the question:
    what is the firm good at doing?

Based on the experiences and research of the ClearLake
partners, the database is maintained and updated regularly.
Each capability is simply described and accompanied by examples of firms exhibiting the capability.

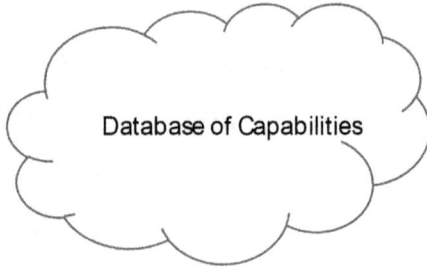

Database of Capabilities

2. A set of **exercises,** both self-directed and guided, to
   compare the firm's situation to the reference database
   and generate the firm's short-list of capabilities, with
   tips on how to apply the resulting awareness to other
   steps of the strategy process

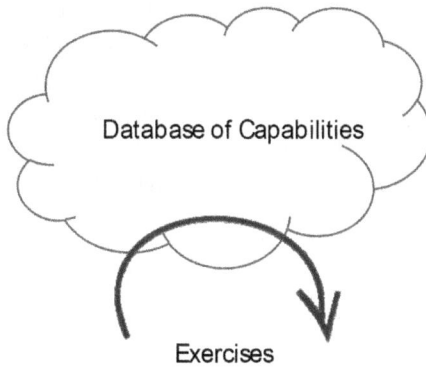

Database of Capabilities

Exercises

SAMPLE CONTENT

Capability is related to values, your core beliefs. How we experience capability is via our worldview and how we make use of that skill. Also knowing why you do what you do, the purpose of your existence.

There are thousands of ways to get things done. There is a poem by Rumi that refers to the many ways to kneel and kiss the ground. Getting things done is not the problem. It is the attitude, the experience, the intention. The thing will get done. Your attitude, experience and intention make the capability more deeply connected with your people.

Because people are not machines. Machines get things done. Robots get things done. People want experiences of joy and love and aliveness, they want meaning. This is where sustainability and creativity happen.

Exercise: What is a capability?

You and your team will have slightly different understandings of what is a capability. In this exercise, we define the ClearLake meaning of the word "capability", with sufficient context and tie-in's to the history of awareness-building.

The exercise includes sharing of points-of-view across the team and relating each member's viewpoint to those of the others using a common language. This effort lays the foundation for subsequent productive dialogue and decision-making.

Exercise: What are the capabilities of my firm?

You and your team are asked to generate your de novo impressions of what the firm does well, typically illustrated using visual aids.

For this exercise, ClearLake has created a proprietary deck of facilitation cards representing the universal set of capabilities. Participants break up into small groups, each with a deck, and assemble clusters of capabilities that best resemble the firm as they know it.

Back in plenary, they read out their results and discuss similarities and differences, and the evidence underlying their points of view. Through iteration, a final set of 5 or 6 capabilities emerges.

Exercise: What do I do with the knowledge?

You and your team take the agreed-upon final set of capabilities into the next step of the strategy process, Create, in which strategic options are defined (see Graphic 3).

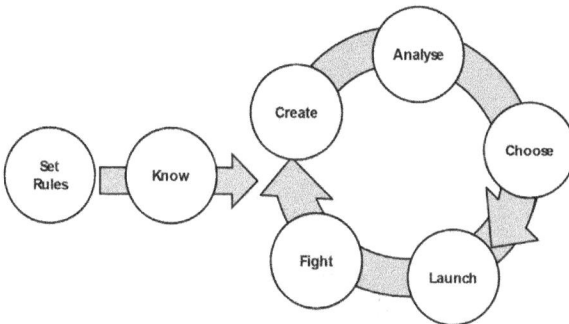

Graphic 3: A better approach to strategy

An awareness of what underlies success will influence your search for ideas, as well as the team discussion of the merits of the individual options. You should not necessarily take any idea off the table based simply on knowing your capabilities. Instead, just keep in mind, and make note of, one additional characteristic of each option: the degree of fit or concordance with the final set of capabilities, to use in the next step of the strategy process, Analyse.

As you draw up each of your strategic options, you put forward an initial assessment of fit (on a scale of 1 to 5, where 5 represents full concordance). Additional analysis may be warranted to test the degree of fit.

When your team gathers to discuss and compare the various strategic options, they can weight the projected financials of each option with the degree of fit. This weighting (0=no fit, 1= perfect fit; e.g. if degree of fit = 3 out of 5, use factor 0.6) takes into account the risk of execution, given that successful execution is less likely in the case of a strategy with a poor fit with existing capabilities.

A risk-adjusted approach provides a better basis for your team's final strategic decision-making, than using an approach devoid of capabilities-based risk adjustment.

Depending on the sophistication of your financial models, you may choose to apply the weighting factor on the Net Present Values, or selectively against specific drivers of the underlying data (e.g. projected growth rates, WACC, etc.).

In the case of strategic options involving M&A, if your internal data systems are sufficiently robust (and brutally honest), you can generate a probability of success (PS) factor based on your company's history of post-merger integration (normalised on a 0:1 scale, where PS=0 represents a history of not meeting acquisition goals and where PS=1 represents a history of meeting all acquisition goals).

For example, some companies (cf. Thomson Reuters) are better at integrating SME-sized acquisitions than large-scale acquisitions, and thus should use different integration PS factors depending on scale.

If you have no readily available data on your ability to integrate acquisitions, you also have the option of analysing and using the PS factor of comparable firms within your industry.

3. A range of custom **workshops** (from one hour in dura-
    tion to a more comprehensive multi-week cross-firm
    process), based on the design principles of June Dela-
    no, co-founder of the ClearLake Group

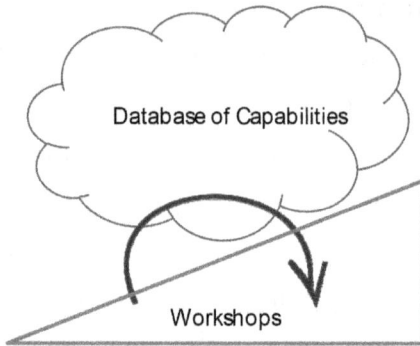

June has designed and facilitated hundreds of strategy
sessions, and stresses the importance of designing executive
learning experiences that make a difference, at the individual,
team and organisational levels. To that end, ClearLake uses
the principles of critical design to build one-of-a-kind programs in collaboration with management.

For example, we assume the best of participants and build on
their strengths. We respect that sophisticated participants deserve
a sophisticated experience, even when their learning needs are basic. We use a variety of frameworks and models, in recognition that
leadership is defined by circumstances and context. We believe in
the power of imagery, metaphors, stories and memorable events

to stimulate and increase engagement, retention and application.

In addition to workshops geared towards corporate strategy teams, we also offer one-on-one and group sessions to support your corporate governance function. As noted earlier, board members should demand capability-level analyses when asked to weigh in on strategic decision-making, and should hold the CEO accountable for the risks associated with choosing strategies with a low fit with existing capabilities.

4. A **community** of practitioners for sharing insights and best practices, comprising

    a.   Our ongoing research initiative (as outlined in the introduction; visit our website www.theclearlakegroup.com for more details)

    b.   Conferences, talks, and seminars (online, in-person)

    c.   Communication on a regular basis about other resources

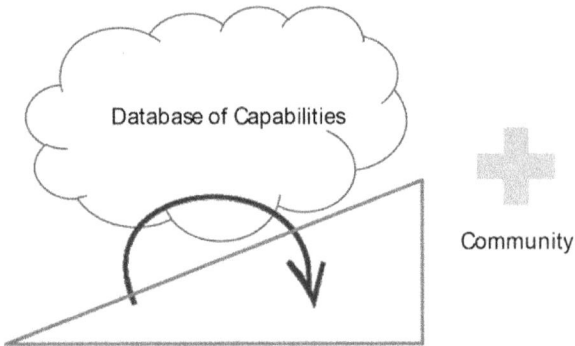

Membership in a community does indeed have its privileges. Everyone who has contributed to or participated in Know Your Capabilities has benefited from responding to the all-too-human curiosity into what makes a firm succeed at one time or another.

Circumstances change and the use of retrospective observations does help to inform future decision-making. Through the Know Your Capabilities global research initiative, we commit to keeping the universal database up-to-date and current, and to making it available to the broader community.

To that end, we use both interactive experiences such as conferences and other means of communication such as newsletters to disseminate the shared learnings of the community.

There is a number of ways by which you can participate as a member of the community, and we welcome your input and inquiries.

AFTERWORD

Any comprehensive writing effort these days must recognise the invaluable role of online resources and the internet. Without access to search engines such as Google and collaborative databases such as Wikipedia, a writer needs much more time for expression. Some of these resources are commercially supported and others are not. Of particular mention, we urge you to donate generously to the Wikimedia Foundation to support them in their efforts (www.wikimedia.org).

In addition to the various sources cited herein, other online tools made light the difficult task of bringing our thoughts to life, tools such as online survey software, collaborative communication and cloud storage services, as well as e-book publishing services. Hats off to all of these innovations.

Many individuals contributed to this book and in particular I would like to acknowledge my co-founders, partners and colleagues at the ClearLake Group. ClearLake comprises a broad virtual network of experts and we are thankful for their collective input to this work, our first full-length publication.

In particular, we'd like to call out the fine talent of Edward Ruehle, business writer and editor, for his patient and thorough overhaul of an early draft of this book. For "writing that strikes a nerve in the market", one should refer to www. edwardruehle.com.

ClearLake itself was founded on the idea that there had to be a better way to create corporate strategy, and that we could draw upon principles of organisation from the natural world. Our inspirations are akin to those of Rachel Armstrong's work in "living architecture", for instance.

And, fortunately, we stand on the shoulders of intellectual giants who have emphasised the importance of capabilities throughout time. Without their original texts and the diligent efforts to translate them into modern language, we would be all the worse off.

You, the reader, face the challenges of forming and revising your company's corporate strategy. To do this, you draw upon talent within and outside the firm, ranging from the rudimentary to the most sophisticated.

At the end of my tour of duty with the strategy consulting firm the Monitor Group, we began to talk about the corporate strategy process as a journey that lasts the lifetime of the firm. In that spirit, I sincerely hope that reading this book helps you on your journey.

As a final example, in Chapter One, we pointed out Thomson Reuters as a great company that appeared to know a couple of its capabilities. As dispassionate observers, we should also consider how much more successful Thomson Reuters would be today if it understood and drew upon its full suite of capabilities.

In its corporate history, Thomson Reuters describes the earliest days of Paul Julius Reuter and how he exploited the new technology of telegraphy to gain advantage through trading commercial information.

Today's version of using such a capability would include exploiting high-speed trading algorithms, as well as social news media such as Twitter, Kakao, or WeChat. If Thomson Reuters knew their capabilities today, they would have invested early in technologies like those, rather than remaining on the sidelines, and letting others take the lead.

We leave you with these words of wisdom:[1]

Therefore I say:

"Know the enemy and know yourself; in a
hundred battles you will never be in peril.

When you are ignorant of the enemy
but know yourself, your chances
of winning or losing are equal.

If ignorant both of your enemy
and of yourself, you are certain in
every battle to be in peril."

ENDNOTES

INTRODUCTION

1. Image of Oliver Ford Davies as Polonius, courtesy of www.bbc.co.uk

CHAPTER ONE

1. Clark, P. and Mills, R. (2013), "Masterminding the Deal", Kogan Page.
2. Leinwand, P. and Mainardi, C. (2010), "The coherence premium", Harvard Business Review.
3. Sheth, J. and Sisodia, R. (2005), "Why good companies fail", European Business Forum, Issue 22, Autumn, pp. 25-30.
4. Chasan, E., "EBay CFO: Making Acquisition Sprees Work", CFO Journal online, the Wall Street Journal, September 12, 2014.

5. Teese, D. (2010) Alfred Chandler and "Capabilities" Theories of Strategy and Management, Industrial and Corporate Change (v. 19, no. 2) pp. 297–316.
6. Prahalad, C.K. and Hamel, G. (1990) The core competence of the corporation, Harvard Business Review (v. 68, no. 3) pp. 79–91.
7. Teece, D., Pisano, G. and Shuen, A. (1997) Dynamic Capabilities and Strategic Management, Strategic Management Journal (v. 18, no. 7) pp. 509–533.
8. Chia, R., MacKay, B. and Masrani, S. (2008) Capabilities as Structuring Disposition: Reframing Core Competencies in Practice Terms, University of St. Andrews School Of Management, PhD thesis.
9. Van der Heijden, K. (1997) Scenarios, Strategies and the Strategy Process, Nijenrode Research Paper Series, Centre for Organisational Learning and Change, No. 1997-01.

CHAPTER TWO

1. http://thelordsofstrategy.com/blog/2010/03/seduced-once-more-by-the-myth-of-corporate-persistence/#more-11

CHAPTER THREE

1. Goleman, D., Boyatzis, R. & A. McKee, Primal Leadership: Learning to Lead with Emotional Intelligence, Harvard Business School Press, 2002.
2. Leinwand, P. and Mainardi, C. (2010), "The coherence premium", Harvard Business Review.
3. Adolph, G., Mainardi, C. and Neely, J. (2012), "The capabilities premium in M&A", Strategy + Business, online.
4. Carroll, P. and Mui, C. (2008), "Billion Dollar Lessons", Portfolio Hardcover.
5. Clark, P. and Mills, R. (2013), "Masterminding the Deal", Kogan Page.
6. Kaplan, R. and Norton, D. (2005), "Creating the Office of Strategy Management", Harvard Business School, Faculty Working Paper, 05-071.
7. Turner, I. (2013) "Corporate Failure", Henley Business School, University of Reading.
8. Ormerod, P., cited in Wilkinson, A. and Mellahi, K. (2005), "Organizational Failure", Long Range Planning, Vol. 38, pp. 235.

9. Sheth, J. and Sisodia, R. (2005), "Why good companies fail", European Business Forum, Issue 22, Autumn, pp. 25-30.

10. Bossidy, L., & Charan, R. (2002). Execution–The discipline of getting things done. New York: Crown Publishing Group.

11. Homburg, C., Krohmer, H., & Workman, Jr., J. P. (2004). A strategy implementation perspective of market orientation. Journal of Business Research, 57(12), 1331–1340.

12. Frigo, M. (2003, March). Strategy or execution. Strategic Finance, 84(9), 9–10.

13. Schaap, J. (2006). Toward strategy implementation success: An empirical study of the role of senior-level leaders in the Nevada gaming industry. UNLV Gaming Research & Review Journal, 10(2), 13–27.

AFTERWORD

1. Sun Tzu, trans. by Samuel Griffith, Chapter III, Offensive Strategy, The Art of War, Oxford University Press, 1963.

www.ingramcontent.com/pod-product-compliance
Lightning Source LLC
Chambersburg PA
CBHW060322220326
41598CB00027B/4398